He's Not Just Teasing!

TEACHER AND COUNSELOR ACTIVITY GUIDE

BOYS TOWN Press®

by Jennifer Licate   Illustrated by Suzanne Beaky

Press

For a Boys Town Press catalog, call **1-800-282-6657**
or visit our website: **BoysTownPress.org**

**All Discussion Questions, Worksheets,
and Activities are available for download.**

ACCESS:
https://www.boystownpress.org/book-downloads

ENTER:
Your first and last names
Email address
Code: 944882hnjtag648
Check "yes" to receive emails to ensure your email link is received.

Printed in the United States
10 9 8 7 6 5 4 3 2 1

Saving Children　Healing Families

Boys Town Press is the publishing division of Boys Town, a
national organization serving children and families.

Table of Contents

TEACHER AND COUNSELOR ACTIVITY GUIDE

Chapter 1
SCHOOL IS HARD

I'M MALCOLM. MOST PEOPLE WOULD DESCRIBE ME AS ATHLETIC. I'm really fast, which gives me an advantage in sports (soccer's my favorite!). I play on as many soccer teams as I can — my community team and my school team. Plus, my friends and I play pick-up games during recess and on weekends. Sports is one area where I feel proud of myself because not everything comes so easily for me.

Sometimes I get in trouble for having extra energy and because I don't like to sit still.

I'd rather be doing something, anything, other than sitting still.

When I was little, everyone thought my high energy was cute. My mom used to say I had two speeds — fast and sleepy. I always considered that a compliment. Who wouldn't want to be fast and have a lot of energy?

My extra energy can often make school tough for me. When I've been sitting awhile, I get bored and want to chat with friends. I'm also not the kid who has all the right answers, and I'm almost always the last one to finish my schoolwork.

I've gotten used to that, but this year has been really hard. My teacher, Mrs. Armstrong, is strict. It feels like she's always calling me out. "Malcolm, stop tapping your pencil." "Malcolm, stop talking." "Malcolm, pay attention."

Sometimes she'll tap my desk when she walks by to remind me to follow her directions. It always feels like I'm getting in trouble for something.

I know a lot of my friends feel the same way, but I definitely get in trouble more often.

I REALLY TRY TO FOLLOW ALL THE RULES.

The problem is, my extra energy sometimes makes me distracted. And when I'm distracted, I'm not paying attention to Mrs. Armstrong's rules. I know I need to be more focused on schoolwork, but it's not easy for me.

The other kids have started to notice how much I get in trouble, too. Nita sits next to me and usually has to remind me to follow Mrs. Armstrong's directions. The other day, I still had my Language Arts workbook out when the class had moved onto journal writing.
Nita giggled and said, "Hello, anyone there? We're doing our journals now."

Laughing it off, I said, "Thanks, I guess I was in outer space." Nita laughed with me. Even though I'm embarrassed when she reminds me to follow directions and stay focused, I know she's trying to help me. Nita's my friend and doesn't want me to get in trouble with Mrs. Armstrong.

The friends I play soccer with sometimes tease me, too. If I miss a ball or make a bad play, they'll imitate Mrs. Armstrong.

"MALCOLM! PAY ATTENTION!" they'll say in their funniest "teacher voice." We all laugh. They know how strict she is, too. Sometimes I get embarrassed when they tease me, but I know they're having fun with me. They're my friends, so it doesn't hurt my feelings.

Follow Up Discussion Questions and Activities

DISCUSSION QUESTIONS

1. What emotions do you think Malcolm is feeling about school this year?

2. What emotions do you think Malcolm is feeling when Nita teases him?

3. What emotions do you think Malcolm is feeling when his friends from soccer tease him?

4. Malcolm laughed off the teasing of Nita and his friends from soccer. Did Malcolm respond well when they teased him?

Ask the students to share their opinions.

Tell the students that we will explore other responses to teasing.

Option A: Malcolm could have gotten upset when Nita and his friends from soccer teased him and told them to mind their own business.

- *Discuss possible outcomes to this option*

Option B: Malcolm could have been quiet when his friends teased him and not said anything.

- *Discuss possible outcomes to this option*

Option C: Malcolm could have gotten upset with his friends from soccer and/or Nita and told them to stop being mean to him.

- *Discuss possible outcomes to this option.*

a. Do your friends ever tease you?

b. What emotions do you feel when your friends tease you?

c. Are there certain friends that hurt your feelings when they tease you but if a different friend teased you in the same way it would not hurt your feelings?

d. What makes teasing okay among friends?

Notes:

Role Play Activity

1. Break students into groups of three students

2. Ask each group to create a scenario where kids tease each other.

   Have examples if groups are having trouble developing an idea (e.g. friend has spaghetti sauce all over his/her face and does not notice, friend trips up the stairs and drops his/her books)

3. Instruct students that the groups will act out their scenario.

4. Instruct students that the students watching each scenario will vote on if the teasing is meant to be funny or mean.

5. Give groups time to create their scenario.

6. Give each group time to act out their scenerio in front of the class.

7. Follow Up Questions (ask students after each scenario is acted out in front of the class)

   • Was this teasing meant to be funny or mean?

   • Why do you feel that way?

8. Allow students to share differing options (explain to students that what may feel mean to one person may feel comfortable to another person)

Self-Reflective Activity

1. Explain to students that we all have strengths and weaknesses. (e.g. Malcolm is a great athlete but he has trouble paying attention in class, and sometimes gets in trouble for this.)

2. Ask each student to make a list of their strengths and weaknesses

3. Explain to students that when you are aware that you have weaknesses, as everyone does, you are less likely to be critical of others' weaknesses.

He's Not Just Teasing!

Strengths and Weaknesses Worksheet

Strengths:

Weaknesses:

Notes:

STRENGTHS AND WEAKNESSES (Continued)

1. **How can I best use my strengths to overcome weakness?**

2. **How can I improve my weeknesses?**

THE CONFRONTATION

I WAS GETTING MORE COMFORTABLE WITH THE SCHOOL YEAR AND FELT LIKE I WAS EVEN DOING BETTER FOLLOWING MRS. ARMSTRONG'S RULES. THEN, A FEW WEEKS AGO, THINGS WENT BAD.

It started when I sat down at the lunch table and Joe blurted out, "Malcolm, what's your deal?"

"What do you mean?" I asked, a little surprised.

"You're always getting in trouble with Mrs. Armstrong. It's like you're clueless. Mrs. Armstrong would probably let us have fun in class and wouldn't be in such a bad mood if we weren't always waiting for you."

I tried to laugh it off. "Yeah right, like Mrs. Armstrong would really let us have fun!"

Joe stared straight into my eyes and coldly said, "She would, if you weren't such an idiot. We're always waiting for you to catch up or stop talking."

Joe was serious. I could tell by the harsh tone in his voice. He wasn't teasing me, and he didn't let me laugh it off. Joe wanted me to know he was really calling me an idiot.

Why didn't any of my friends defend me? It made me feel like they were all against me. Does everyone think I'm an idiot? I've never thought of myself as smart, but I'm not an idiot either. Or am I? What if Joe is right? I'm slow to finish my schoolwork, and I'm always getting in trouble. No one gets in trouble as much as I do.

Joe's rude comment bothered me, but I tried to brush it off. The problem was, I couldn't brush it off. This felt different. It wasn't like when Nita and my other friends messed with me. I knew they were just teasing. I knew my friends liked me and wouldn't want to hurt my feelings. BUT JOE WASN'T TEASING. HE WAS BEING MEAN. JOE WASN'T MY FRIEND.

Over the next few weeks, Joe continued to make mean comments. He took every opportunity to embarrass me. Whenever Mrs. Armstrong stopped class to remind me to stay on task, Joe rolled his eyes or smirked in an exaggerated way so everyone noticed.

He even snickered every time Mrs. Armstrong walked by and tapped my shoulder or my desk to remind me to pay attention. It got to the point where Joe said something rude to me every single day, multiple times a day. And, just like the first time it happened, no one defended me or told Joe to stop.

Did my friends think Joe was just teasing and I'm okay with it, or did they agree with him? Either way, I didn't deserve to be treated that way.

IT WAS SO FRUSTRATING!

One day, because I was late for class, I ran up the stairs.

I TRIPPED ON THE LAST STEP AND DROPPED MY BOOKS.

Joe saw me and laughed.

"Ha, Ha! Malcolm is at it again. Didn't you learn how to walk when you were a baby? Maybe you need to go back to nursery school."

"Joe, give it a rest," I yelled. "Your comments about me ruining class and messing up are bothering me. I get your message, but you keep saying the same thing. **Can you just stop?"**

Joe looked at me with a smug smile and said, "Then don't do anything stupid that I need to point out."

I felt sad and defeated because I knew that was impossible. Everyone makes mistakes. I'm no different. I make mistakes. Actually, I make lots of mistakes.

I was proud of myself for having the courage to stand up to Joe and asking him to stop. But it didn't help. In fact, it gave Joe another opportunity to be mean to me. My only hope was that Joe would think about what I said and feel bad about hurting my feelings. Maybe that would be enough for him to stop making mean comments.

CHAPTER TWO

Follow Up Discussion Questions and Activities

DISCUSSION QUESTIONS

1. What emotions do you think Malcolm was feeling when Joe confronted him during lunch?

2. Do you think Malcolm handled the confrontation with Joe during lunch well?

3. Malcolm tried to laugh off Joe's comments during lunch. Do you think Malcolm responded well to Joe's comments?

Ask students to share their opinions.

1. What is another way Malcolm could have handled this confrontation?

   Option A: Malcolm could have been quiet and not responded to Joe's comments.

   Discuss possible outcomes to this option.

   Option B: Malcolm could have yelled at Joe to stop being a jerk and to worry about himself instead of what he (Malcolm) is doing.

   Discuss possible outcomes to this option.

   Option C: Malcolm could have gotten upset and stormed out of the lunchroom.

   Discuss possible outcomes to this option.

2. Do you think Joe's intent during lunch was to be funny or mean?

3. What emotions do you think Malcolm was feeling when he asked Joe to stop making these comments?

4. What emotions do you think Malcolm was feeling when Joe refused to stop?

Notes:

Writing & Drawing Activity

- Think of a time that you wished you had stood up to a friend/classmate who made comments to you that hurt your feelings.

- Write what you would say to this friend/classmate to stand up for yourself.

- Draw how you would confront this friend/classmate, similar to how comics show one scene to the next.

WRITING WORKSHEET

Think of a time that you wished you had stood up to a friend/classmate who made comments to you that hurt your feelings.

WRITE: What you would say to this friend/classmate to stand up for yourself?

____

____

____

____

____

____

____

____

____

____

____

____

____

He's Not Just Teasing!

He's Not Just Teasing!

Drawing Worksheet

DRAW: How you would confront this friend/classmate, similar to how comics show one scene to the next.

<table>
<tr><td>

</td><td>

</td></tr>
<tr><td>

</td><td>

</td></tr>
<tr><td>

</td><td>

</td></tr>
</table>

He's Not Just Teasing!

TEACHER AND COUNSELOR ACTIVITY GUIDE

Chapter 3
The Worst Day

I tried to stay hopeful at school. At recess, I played soccer with my friends like always.

I was playing well. I love it when I have games like that. I had a break-away opportunity and dribbled the ball right in front of the goal. I kicked the ball hard toward the net, thinking I'd score, but the ball sailed way too high and went over the playground's wooden fence. No one's allowed to go beyond the fence, so we had no ball for the rest of recess. I felt terrible and knew everyone would be annoyed.

I looked at all my soccer buddies and sheepishly said, "Sorry."

"MALCOLM! PAY ATTENTION!" squawked Anthony in his funniest teacher's voice. We all started laughing. All of us except Joe. He glared at me and snapped,

"Oh great, Malcolm! Can't you do anything right?"

I looked away and said nothing, hoping he'd calm down and stop yelling. He didn't.

"Malcolm, you ruined our game. It's bad enough you ruin class, but do you have to ruin recess too?"

I was too embarrassed to look at him or respond. So I looked around at my friends, hoping someone would defend me. No one did.

"That's it," Joe screamed. "You can't play soccer with us anymore. Go play with the girls. You can ruin their game!"

Just then recess ended, and we all lined up to return to class.

I was so angry walking back into school. How could Joe say that to me?

It's bad enough he makes me feel insecure in class, but now he's taking all the fun out of playing soccer with my friends.

And why didn't any of my friends defend me?
Do they agree with Joe? I thought they liked playing
sports with me. Guess I was wrong. If they wanted
me to stay on the soccer team, they would've said
something. Maybe they aren't even my friends? Real
friends would defend me. I would've defended them
if anyone screamed at them the way Joe yelled at me.
If I don't have any friends and can't even play soccer
during recess, it'll be torture! I might as well never
come to school again.

All day I kept thinking about how I could fix
this, but I couldn't come up with a solution. No one
talked to me about what happened at recess or even
noticed how quiet I was the rest of the school day.
I still felt sad and angry when I got home,

so I slammed the front door as hard as I could. I didn't
even care if it broke.

I WAS THAT ANGRY!

Panicked, my mom rushed into the room and
yelled, "What in the world is going on?" She took one
look at my face and knew something was very wrong.
She kneeled beside me and softly asked, "What's
wrong? What happened at school today?"

"School's the Worst!"

I shouted.

"I don't wanna go back again!"

"Oh, Malcolm, I'm sorry you had a bad day. Lemme get you a snack. Sit down and take a few minutes to calm down. When you're ready, we'll talk about what happened and figure something out."

I sat down at the table and just fumed.

I didn't know how this could get any better.

Follow Up Discussion Questions and Activities

Discussion Questions

1. What emotions do you think Malcolm was feeling when he was playing soccer with his friends?

2. What emotions do you think Malcolm was feeling when he kicked the soccer ball over the fence?

3. What emotions do you think Malcolm was feeling when his friends teased him for kicking the ball over the fence?

4. What emotions do you think Malcolm was feeling when Joe yelled at him for ruining the game?

5. Malcolm was silent when Joe yelled at him for ruining the soccer game. Do you think Malcolm responded well?

Allow students to share differing opinions.

1. What other options did Malcolm have?

   Option A: Malcolm gets angry and tells Joe that he's is a terrible soccer player and he can't decide who can play soccer and who cannot play.

   Discuss possible outcomes to this option.

   Option B: Malcolm gets upset and runs away from the confrontation during the soccer game.

   Discuss possible outcomes to this option.

   Option C: Malcolm listens to Joe's comments during the soccer game. Later, Malcolm yells at his friends for not defending him against Joe's comments.

   Discuss possible outcomes to this option.

2. Why do you think Malcolm's friends didn't defend him when Joe yelled at him for ruining the game?

3. Who do you talk to when you have a bad day?

4. Have you witnessed another kid being yelled at in front of a group of his/her peers?

5. Has this ever happened to you?

6. What could Malcolm's friends have done to stop Joe from yelling at Malcolm?

Notes:

____

____

____

____

ACTIVITIES

Writing Activity

- Instruct the students to write in their journal that evening from the perspective they chose, sharing their feelings and thoughts about what happened during recess.

He's Not Just Teasing!

WRITING WORKSHEET

Write your feelings and thoughts about what happened during recess.

Self-Reflective Activity

- Share with the students that Malcolm felt like he had no friends.

- Ask students: Have you ever felt like you had no friends? How did you get through this time to feel better?

- Instruct the students: Reflect on this through any means you are comfortable. (e.g. write a story about it, list the steps you took to resolve the conflict, draw a picture of how you felt).

SELF-REFLECTIVE WORKSHEET

WRITE A STORY OR MAKE A LIST:

____

____

____

____

____

____

____

____

DRAW A PICTURE OF HOW YOU FELT:

He's Not Just Teasing!

AM I BEING BULLIED?

AFTER A BIT, MOM HANDED ME A SNACK AND SAT DOWN. SHE LOOKED WORRIED.

"Start from the beginning," she said calmly. "I wanna know why you're so upset."

I told her all about Joe. I told her how he had made a few mean comments, but now he makes them all the time.

"Joe calls me an idiot and says I ruin class because Mrs. Armstrong has to wait for me. He rolls his eyes or laughs when she tells me to stop talking. Joe says mean stuff and laughs at me in front of my friends, and they never defend me. It's embarrassing and makes me feel like a loser."

Then, with tears in my eyes, I told Mom about what went down during recess.

"I'M NEVER GONNA BE ABLE TO PLAY SOCCER WITH MY FRIENDS AGAIN."

"I DON'T EVER WANNA GO BACK TO THAT SCHOOL!"

I shouted in despair.

"Oh, honey, I'm so sorry this happened to you." Then I got a Mom hug. "I know school is hard for you. You're just an active kid that would rather be moving. You'll love that about yourself when you're older," Mom promised, and then she said Joe was a bully.

"Mom! Joe isn't a bully, he's just a big jerk!"

"Malcolm, have you ever asked Joe to stop?"

"I asked him to stop, Mom, but he didn't. He even called me an idiot and told me he'd have nothing to say if I stopped doing stupid stuff. He made me feel like it was all my fault."

"Well, it's definitely not your fault. Joe's wrong!" Mom declared.

Mom went on to explain the difference between teasing and bullying. She said friends tease each other so no one takes themselves too seriously.

We all make mistakes, and it's good to be able to laugh
at our slip-ups instead of getting upset and being hard
on ourselves. Friends also tease each other about the
way they act around other people. If you're making a
mistake, friendly teasing can teach you a lesson.
I didn't really understand what Mom meant, so I
asked her to explain it again.

"Well, say you had spaghetti sauce on your
chin. Friends would probably tease you about being
a sloppy eater and then you would try to be more
careful the next time you ate. Teasing is your friends'
way of teaching you how to do something better,"
she said.

Mom described how teasing is very different
from bullying, and it made sense. I remembered the
times when Nita and my other pals teased me about
not paying attention or missing a play in soccer. Even
though I was embarrassed, I was always able to laugh
about it with them. Teasing from friends feels a lot
different than what Joe said. I knew my friends were
just trying to be funny and encourage me to change
my behavior. I also knew they cared about me and
weren't trying to hurt my feelings.

"Malcolm, you asked Joe to stop. If Joe was
teasing, he would have stopped when you asked
him, even if he initially thought he was being funny.

Teasing isn't meant to be hurtful. It's supposed to be a lighthearted way for friends to encourage each other or improve their behaviors and not repeat mistakes."

"Bullying is about embarrassing others and putting them down to make the bully look better. It never works. Bullies always look mean," Mom said.

"Also, Joe makes mean comments every day. It's a pattern for him. That's another sign that he's been bullying you. Bullying is a pattern of behavior, not a one-time remark."

Follow Up Discussion Questions and Activities

DISCUSSION QUESTIONS

1. As you heard about Joe, did you think he was a bully?
   - Why? or Why Not?

2. What is the difference between a bully and a kid who makes mean comments?

3. Were you surprised to learn about negative teasing, that there is a description for this kind of teasing among friends?

4. Has the teasing among your friends ever gone too far and hurt your feelings?
   - Would anyone like to share an example of this?

Drawing Activity

- Draw a picture of yourself, showing how you feel when you have a bad day.

- On this same paper, draw what makes you feel better when you have a bad day (e.g. drawing, listening to music, playing outside, talking to parent/guardian, writing your thoughts in a journal).

He's Not Just Teasing!

DRAWING WORKSHEET

Draw a picture of yourself, showing how you feel when you have a bad day:

Draw what makes you feel better when you have a bad day: (e.g. drawing, listening to music, playing outside, talking to parent/guardian, writing your thoughts in a journal).

He's Not Just Teasing!

Role Play Activity

- Break students into groups of 4 to 5 students.

- Ask students to create a scenario where one student is bullying another student.

- The other students in the scenario will defend the victim of bullying, so they are not bystanders to bullying.

- Instruct the students to include what the bully will say, how the victim will respond and how the other kids in the scenario will defend the victim.

ROLE PLAY WORKSHEET

What will the bully say?:

____

____

____

____

How will the victim respond?:

____

____

____

____

How will the other kids help defend the victim?:

____

____

____

____

He's Not Just Teasing!

TEACHER AND COUNSELOR ACTIVITY GUIDE

Chapter 5
RESOLUTION

MOM WANTED TO MAKE ME FEEL BETTER AND HELP FIND A SOLUTION TO MY PROBLEM, SO SHE ASKED WHO ELSE PLAYS SOCCER WITH JOE AND ME DURING RECESS. I started naming the other guys and when I said Carlos, Mom interrupted me.

"Malcolm, what if you ask Carlos to stick up for you during tomorrow's recess? You and Carlos have been friends since kindergarten. I'm sure he doesn't want you kicked out."

"MOM, HE'LL THINK I'M A WIMP IF I ASK HIM TO STICK UP FOR ME!"

"No, he won't," Mom assured me. "He's such a nice boy. We all need our friends' support, especially when we're going through hard times."

Mom did have a point. All the guys like Carlos. If he tells Joe he wants me to play soccer, Joe will listen. Maybe it'll make Joe stop messing with me so much, too? It's worth a try.

"Malcolm, you have soccer practice with Carlos tonight. You really should talk to him," urged Mom.

I was nervous to ask Carlos to defend me, but I wanted things to get better, so I took Mom's advice. I approached Carlos as he was walking off the field after practice.

"Carlos, what'd you think about what happened at recess?" I asked.

I had no idea how Carlos felt or what he was about to say. Would he agree with Joe? Or would he think Joe was rude? "That was so not cool.

Joe completely overreacted, like he always does," Carlos answered.

I was so relieved Carlos agreed with me that I excitedly said, "I don't want to stop playing with you guys because playing soccer during recess is awesome!"

"You should definitely keep playing with us.

Don't let Joe scare you.
I'll have your back, and I'll tell Joe you're playing.
If he doesn't like it, too bad."

"Thanks, Carlos!"

From then on, whenever Joe was rude or said something mean, Carlos defended me no matter where we were or what we were doing. My other friends started to defend me, too. It felt good to have their support.

I also started standing up for myself. I was nervous at first, but each time I defended myself I gained more confidence to stand up to Joe. It made me feel strong and a little more in control of the situation. When Joe realized I wouldn't back down and the other kids didn't like how he was speaking to me, he eventually stopped.

Once the bullying ended, I realized just how much it hurt and affected me. I was always worried about the next comment from Joe and how I'd deal with it. I'm glad I took my mom's advice. If I hadn't, the bullying may have continued or even gotten worse. I thought I could deal with it on my own. But having a friend's support helped me develop the confidence I needed to stand up for myself.

I was so happy. I didn't even have to ask Carlos to defend me, he offered. Joe couldn't bully me anymore if I had my friend's support, right? Maybe Carlos's support would get my other friends to defend me, too? I was feeling hopeful, maybe this was the solution I needed.

The next day at recess, as I walked toward the soccer field, Joe's voice thundered through the air.

"OH, NO, NO, NO!"

he yelled.

"WE'RE NOT HAVING YOU RUIN ANOTHER GAME FOR US."

"NOPE, I'M PLAYING,"

I said confidently and with no hesitation.

"Joe, give it a rest," added Carlos.

"It was one ball over the fence. He's playing! You're just worried Malcolm will beat you."

All the other guys started laughing. I guess Joe didn't want to challenge everyone, so he just shrugged his shoulders and said rather lamely, "Fine, but don't say I didn't warn you when he ruins another game."

Joe still isn't one of my favorite people. In fact, I still think he's a jerk.

But we can be around each other and still have fun. He doesn't get in my face and make mean comments anymore.

If I hear him say something negative toward someone else, I'm quick to confront him. I know how terrible I felt when I was bullied.

I DON'T WANT ANYONE ELSE TO FEEL THAT WAY. BULLYING IS WRONG.

Follow Up Discussion Questions and Activities

Discussion Questions

1. Malcolm dealt with Joe's bullying by asking a friend for support against the bullying. What is another way Malcolm could have dealt with the bullying?

   Option A: Malcolm could have yelled at Joe every time he bullied him and told Joe to leave him alone and told Joe that he is a bully.

   Discuss possible outcomes of this option.

   Option B: Malcolm could have ignored the bullying and hoped for it to stop.

   Discuss possible outcomes of this option.

   Option C: Malcolm could have left this whole friend group to get away from the bullying and try to make friends with another group of friends.

   Discuss possible outcomes of this option.

2. What characteristics does someone possess, that allows them to stand up to a bully?

   - Do you think you would defend a friend against a bully?

3. Have you ever seen someone get bullied or treated badly?

    • How did you respond?

4. Have you ever dealt with bullying, personally?

Encouraging Change Activity

- Find a classmate that is not often included.

- Invite that classmate to join you to play at recess, or to join your lunch table.

- Explain to students that when kids are included, they are less likely to be a victim of bullying.

- Tell students to pay attention to how they feel when they include others, it should make them feel good.

He's Not Just Teasing!

ENCOURAGING CHANGE WORKSHEET

GOAL:

Steps to follow to reach goal:

Notes:

He's Not Just Teasing!

Class Project Activity

- Through a class discussion, make a list of the differences and similarities of teasing and bullying (consider using a venn diagram).

- Instruct the students to copy this list to a place where they could easily reference the list.

He's Not Just Teasing!

CLASS PROJECT WORKSHEET

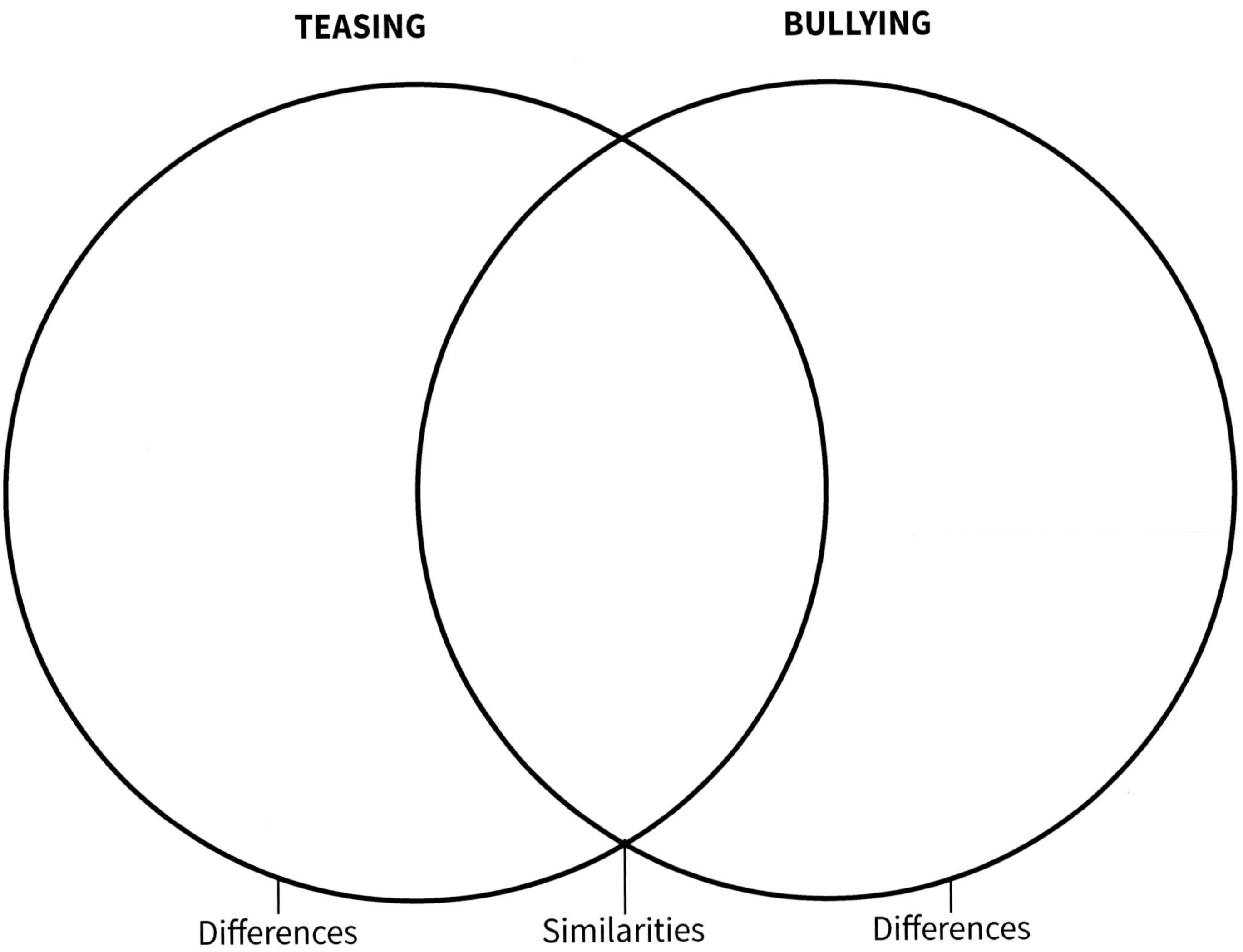

TEASING   **BULLYING**

Differences   Similarities   Differences

Notes:

He's Not Just Teasing!

Boys Town Press books
Kid-friendly books for teaching social skills

A book series and accompanying activity guides focused on changing friendships, finding your place, advocating for yourself, and being true to who you are.

978-1-944882-63-1

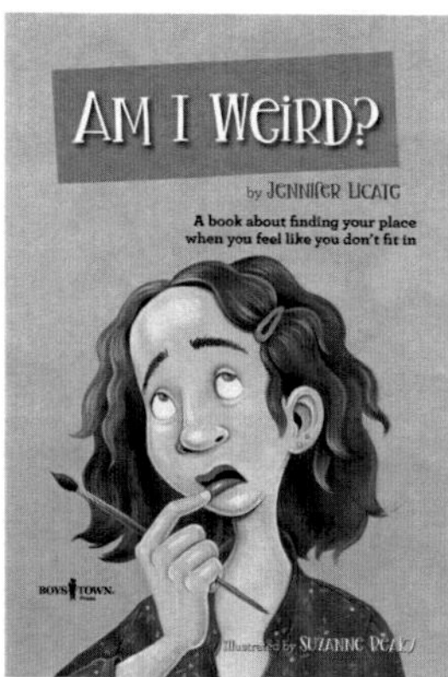

978-1-944882-65-5

978-1-944882-67-9

978-0-938510-68-0

Navigating Friendships

Jennifer Licate
GRADES 4-7

978-1-944882-64-8

978-1-944882-66-2

978-1-944882-68-6

978-0-938510-69-7

A book series teaching important lessons about lying, cheating, and being a good friend.

978-1-934490-94-5

978-1-944882-03-7

978-1-944882-10-5

978-1-944882-21-1

978-1-944882-32-7

BoysTownPress.org

For information on Boys Town, its Education Model®, Common Sense Parenting®, and training programs: boystowntraining.org, boystown.org/
parentingtraining@BoysTown.org, 1-800-545-5771
For parenting and educational books and other resources:
BoysTownPress.org, btpress@BoysTown.org, 1-800-282-6657